MEMOIRS

OF THE

BOSTON SOCIETY OF NATURAL HISTORY.

I. Volcanic Manifestations in New England: *being an enumeration of the principal Earthquakes from* 1638 *to* 1869. By William T. Brigham, A.M.

Read April 7th, 1869.

ALTHOUGH no recent or noteworthy manifestation of either seismic or volcanic force has made the present an especially appropriate time to review the records of the past, and collect the scattered and imperfect accounts of such seismic phenomena as have been noticed in New England in the comparatively short period covered by the observation of civilized nations, yet the steadily increasing interest in these studies will, perhaps, render useful a compilation of such facts as possess historical authenticity, which may serve as a basis for the observations which must be made in the field.

M. Alexis Perrey, the distinguished savant of Dijon, has published[1] in his series of local catalogues a tolerably complete list of the earthquakes which are said to have taken place in the central and eastern part of North America, but his work is not easily obtained. Professor Williams, also, in the Memoirs of the American Academy,[2] has collected much valuable material; and Professor Mallet's catalogue,[3] and many fragmentary scientific and historical papers contain nearly all the rest that is known of the surface indications of that power which has in ages long past done so much to mould the surface of New England.

Indian tradition gives us nothing of any value, for people in an uncivilized state do not note the paroxysmal changes of Nature, though the weather signs are often carefully observed. The early settlers in New England were men of little leisure, whose whole life was a battle against stubborn nature and sinful man, and the earthquake shock was a slight thing beside the abundant harvest of a cornfield, or the erection of the town stocks. Where the hand of the Lord led them they were willing to go, and where His hand was seen in the tremor of the mighty earth a record was made, but much as the record of some pest, or a great drought.

[1] Annales de la Societé d'Emulation des Vosges, t. VII, 2 cah. 1850.

[2] Memoirs of the American Academy of Arts and Sciences, vol. I, p. 260. 1785.

[3] Catalogue of Recorded Earthquakes, from 1606 B. C. to A. D. 1850. 1853.

1638. Eighteen years after the Pilgrims landed at Plymouth they felt the first earthquake most of them had ever experienced. In Bradford's History is the following account:[1]

"This year (1638) aboute ye 1. or 2. of June was a great & fearfull earthquake; it was in this place heard before it was felte. It came with a rumbling noyse, or low murmure like unto remoate thunder: it came from ye norward, & pased southward. As ye noyse aproched nerer, the earth begane to shake and came at length with that violence as caused platters, dishes, & such like things as stoode upon shelves, to clatter and fall downe; yea persons were afraid of ye houses them selves. It so fell oute y^t^ at ye same time diverse of ye cheefe of this towne were mett together at one house, conferring with some of their friends that were upon their removall from ye place, (as if ye Lord would herby show ye signs of his displeasure, in their shaking a peeces & removalls one from an other.) However it was very terrible for ye time, and as ye men were set talking in ye house, some women & others were without ye doors, and ye earth shooke with y^t^ violence as they could not stand without catching hould of ye posts & pails y^t^ stood next them; but ye violence lasted not long. And about halfe an hower, or less, came an other noyse & shaking, but nether so loud nor strong as ye former, but quickly passed over, and so it ceased. It was not only on ye seacoast, but ye Indeans felt it within land; and some ships that were upon ye coast were shaken by it. So powerfull is ye mighty hand of ye Lord, as to make both the earth & sea to shake, and the mountaines to tremble before him when he pleases; and who can stay his hand? It was observed that ye somers, for divers yeares togeather after this earthquake were not so hot & seasonable for ye ripning of corne & other fruits as formerly; but more could & moyst, & subject to erly & untimely frosts, by which, many times, much Indean corne came not to maturitie; but whether this was any cause, I leave it to naturallists to judge."

Johnson, in his "Wonder-working Providence of Sion's Saviour in New England,"[2] describes the event as follows, and it will be noticed that his account adds several particulars to that of Bradford:

"This yeare, the first day of the Fourth Month, about two of the clock in the afternoone, the Lord caus'd a great and terrible Earthquake, which was general throughout all the English Plantations; the motion of the earth was such, that it caused divers men (that had never known an Earthquake before) being at work in the Fields, to cast downe their working tooles, and run with gastly, terrified lookes, to the next company they could meet withall; it came from the Westerne and uninhabited parts of this Wildernesse, and went the direct course."

Winthrop[3] fixes the time of day a little later and gives some vivid details. He says: "Between three and four in the afternoon, being clear, warm weather, the wind westerly, there was a great earthquake. It came with a noise like a continued thunder, or the rattling of coaches in London, but was presently gone. It was at Connecticut, at Narragansett, at Pascataquack, and all the parts round about. It shook the ships which rode in the harbor, and all the islands. The noise and the shakings continued about four minutes. The earth was unquiet twenty days after by times." Had there been observers farther to the north and west we might have learned more of the extent of territory shaken and the direction of the vibrations; but so little interest did natural phenomena excite in those days — unless indeed they could be connected with some poor witch, or used as weapons by the belligerent clergy, — that the scanty records remaining do not give much information of any value. One historian says the vibration seemed to come from the north, another from the west. There were two shocks, and the paroxysm ended in a series of feeble vibrations extending over twenty days.

[1] Page 366, Edition of the Massachusetts Historical Society.

[2] Chap. XII. Chap. V, p. 107, Poole's Edition.

[3] Vol. I, p. 265, Savage's Edition.

March 5, 1642–3, "At seven in the morning, it being the Lord's day, there was
a great earthquake. It came with a rumbling noise like the former, but through 1642-3.
the Lord's mercy it did no harm." [1] Governor Winthrop seems to be the only one of our early historians who notices this earthquake; neither Mallet nor Von Hoff include it in their catalogues.

From the town records of Newbury we have the following:

June 1st. "Being this day assembled to treat or consult together about the well ordering of the affairs of the towne, about one of the clocke in the afternoone, the sunn shining faire, it pleased God suddenly to raise a vehement earthquake, coming with a shrill clap of thunder, issuing, as is supposed, out of the east, which shook the earth and the foundations of the house in a very violent manner to our great amazement and wonder, wherefore taking notice of so great and strange a hand of God's providence, we were desirous of leaving it on record to the view of after ages, to the intent that all might take notice of Almighty God and feare his name."

A very slight shock was noticed in 1653 (October 29), but did not attract general notice, and is not mentioned by Mallet in his catalogue. Five years later 1653.
occurred what is usually styled in the old histories, "a great earthquake." Morton says,[2] "This year there was a very great earthquake in New England," but no 1658.
account of the day, hour or direction is given; perhaps it was April 4.[3] Von Hoff[4] enumerates this in his list, but gives no further particulars, referring simply to the Philosophical Transactions as his authority; Mallet does the same.[5] The same obscurity is over the "great" earthquake of January 31, 1660, which is referred to in Professor
Williams's paper already quoted. 1660.

January 26, 1662, three violent shocks were felt in New England; chimneys
were thrown down. *November* 6, another in the same place. 1662.

February 5, *N. S.* Morton tells us that "at the shutting in of the evening,
there was a very great earthquake in New England, and the same night another, 1663.
although something less than the former, and again on the seventh of the same month there was another about nine of the clock in the morning." [6] This earthquake was severer in Canada than in the plantations of Massachusetts Bay, and Charlevoix assures us that trees were uprooted, chasms opened, and the course of rivers changed.[7] Clavigero, in his "History of Mexico," [8] declares that it overwhelmed a chain of mountains of freestone more than two hundred miles long, and changed that large tract into a plain; and this has a singular confirmation in the "Journal des Sçavans," [9] where, in a review of the life of the celebrated Mary of the Incarnation, Superior of the Ursulines at Quebec, written by her son, is the following passage:

"Ce tremblement agita plus de quatrecent lieuës de païs. Tadoussaç, Quebec, Sillery, les trois Rivieres, Montreal, les Hiroquois, l'Acadie, et la Nouvelle Holland en ressentirent les secousses * * *. Les effets en furent si terrible et si prodigieux, qu'on auroit de la peine à les lire même dans ce Livre et beaucoup plus à les croire, s'ils n'étoient arrivez de nos jours, et s'ils n'avoient pour temoins une infinité d'habitans de tous ces

[1] Winthrop's History of New England, vol. II, edition of 1853, p. 112.

[2] Memorial, p. 276.

[3] Canadian Naturalist and Geologist, vol. V, p. 369.

[4] Chronik der Erdbeben und Vulcan-ausbrüche, I, p. 307.

[5] Philosophical Transactions, vol. L, p. 9.

[6] Morton's Memorial, p. 289.

[7] Charlevoix Histoire de la Nouvelle France. A mountain was thrown on to the Isle aux Coudres. See pp. 93, 95, vol. I, English Translation. Paul Dudley gives the year 1662. Philosophical Transactions, XXXIX, p. 64. See Von Hoff Geschichte der Erdoberfläche, t. II, p. 542.

[8] I have been unable to find the passage referred to.

[9] Vol. VII, May, 1678, p. 103.

païs qui vivent encore. L'on voyoit des montagnes s'entrechoquer, d'autres se jettoient dans le grand Fleuve de Saint Laurent; quelques autres se sont enfoncées dans la terre. Il y en a eu qui se sont detachées de leurs fondemens, et qui ont avancé plus de cent brasses dans le Fleuve portant et retenant leurs arbres et leur verdure. Les Montagnes des deux côtez se sont perduës et égalées aux Campagnes voisines plus d'une lieuë sur le Fleuve, et il y a un espace de plus de cent lieuës tout rempli de rochers et de montagnes qui s'est tellement applani, qu'il fait aujourd'hui une grande plaine aussi égale que si elle avoit été dressé au niveau. On voit depuis ce tems-la des Montagnes où il n'y en avoit jamais eu; des Rivieres où il y avoit auparavant des Forêts, et on trouve des Lacs et des Fleuves où l'on voyait des Montagnes inaccessibles."

No contradiction followed the publication of this remarkable statement in Paris. The substance of Charlevoix's account is as follows: About half past five in the evening, the heavens being very serene, there was suddenly heard a roar, like that of a great fire. Immediately the buildings were shaken violently, and doors opened and shut of themselves with a great slamming. Bells rung without being touched, and walls split asunder, while the floors separated and fell down. The fields were raised "like precipices," and mountains seemed to be moving out of their place. Animals were terrified and uttered strange cries. For nearly half an hour the trembling lasted, a most unusual time, but it began to abate in a quarter of an hour after it first began. The same evening, about eight o'clock, there was another equally violent shock, and within half an hour two others less violent. The next day, "about three hours from the morning, there was a violent shock, which lasted a long time; and the next night some counted thirty-two shocks; of which many were violent." Nor did these earthquakes cease until the July following.[1] New England and New York were shaken, as well as Canada, but in a less degree, and the whole territory convulsed, so far as can be learned, extended nearly three hundred miles from east to west, and half as many from north to south. Sometimes the shocks were sudden, at other times they came on gradually; some seemed to be vertical, others undulatory. Springs and brooks were dried up, or became sulphurous; and some had their channel so completely altered as hardly to be recognized. Between Tadoussac and Quebec "two mountains" were shaken into the St. Lawrence, and perhaps from a similar accession of material the Island Aux Coudres became larger than it was before. The course of all these waves was from the northwest when felt in New England, and the centre of disturbance was not far from the ancient volcano of Montreal. On the shores of Massachusetts Bay, houses were shaken so that pewter fell from the shelves, and the tops of several chimneys were broken; but as many of the latter were of rough stone, they were the more easily overthrown.[2]

From the Newbury record is the following: "January 26th. There was an earthquake at the shutting in of the evening." One of the greatest in New England; and on February 5th another. The first shock continued about half an hour. On the same day, at evening, another, and they did not cease till July following.[3]

1665. *February* 24, 1665. In the neighborhood of Tadoussac and La Malbaye, in Canada, violent shocks were felt, but they are hardly noticed in any of the New England chronicles. Lallemant is the authority for this, and also for an earthquake on

[1] Memoirs of the American Academy, vol. I, p. 264.

[2] See also Frezier's Voyage, pp. 210, 211. Also MacGregor's Travels in America.

[3] Coffin's History of Newbury, p. 66. Probably the date February 5, is simply a mistake from the change of style. February 5, N. S., is the same as January 26, O. S.

October 15th of the same year, at 9^h $30'$ P.M., preceded by a noise louder than that of two hundred pieces of artillery, and lasting "about the time of a Miserere."[1]

Earthquakes are mentioned in the years 1668, 1669, 1670 and 1706, but no account has been preserved.[2] Neither Mallet nor Von Hoff mention them. Dr. Mather simply speaks of those occurring in the last two years, and there was one on *January* 8, **1720.**
1720, but all were so slight as to escape general notice, and no particulars have been recorded.

November 8, 1727. About forty minutes past ten o'clock in the evening, during **1727.**
a perfect calm, clear air and serene sky, a heavy rumbling noise was heard. At first far off, it grew louder and in about thirty seconds the shock came. Houses shook and rocked as if falling to pieces. Pewter and china were thrown from their shelves. Stone walls and chimneys were shaken down, and it was difficult for men to stand up. The ground seemed to rise and fall as the vibration passed. The shock commenced about half a minute from the time the noise was first heard, rose to its maximum in about a minute, and then decreased in half a minute. The direction was from northwest to southeast. At Newbury, and about the mouth of the Merrimack River, the shock was most violent. Reverend Benjamin Colman, D.D., says:[3] "There the earth opened and threw up many cart-loads of a fine sand and ashes, mixed with some small remains of sulphur; but so small that taking up some of it in my fingers and dropping it into a chaffing-dish of bright coals, in a dark place, once in three times the blue flame of the sulphur would plainly arise and give a small scent, and but a small one. By this it seems evident that it was a sulphurous blast which burst open the ground and threw up the calcined bituminous earth." In the account Dr. Dudley sent to the Royal Society,[4] the sulphurous smell is spoken of, and he says: "Persons of credit do also affirm that just before, or at the time of the earthquake, they perceived flashes of light."

An account written by Stephen Jaques is as follows:[5]

> "On the twenty-ninth day of October, between ten and eleven, it being sabath day night, there was a terabel earthquake. The like was never known in this land. It came with a dreadful roreing, as if it was thunder, and then a pounce like grate guns two or three times close one after another. It shook down bricks from ye tops of abundance of chimnies, some allmost all the heads. . . . All that was about ye houses trembled, beds shook, some cellar walls fell partly down. Benjamins Plumer's stone without his dore fell into his cellar. Stone wals fell in a hundred plasis. Most peopel gat up in a moment. It came very often all ye night aftar, and it was heard two or three times some days and nights, and on the sabath day night on ye twenty-fourth of December following, between ten and eleven, it was very loud, as any time except ye first, and twice that night aftar but not so loud. The first night it broke out in more than ten places in ye town in ye clay low land, blowing up ye sand, sum more, sum less. In one place near Spring Island it blew out, as was judged twenty loads, and when it was cast on coals in ye night, it burnt like brimstone."

Probably the smell of brimstone noticed was purely imaginary, and the earth or sand thrown out was due to the agency of water pent up beneath the clay soil, since, as will be seen below, the water which issued with it continued to flow for several days.

1 Relation de ce qui s'est passé de plus remarquables aux missions des Péres de la Compagnie de Jésus en la Nouvelle France en 1664 et 1665. Par Jérome Lallemant. p. 115 et suiv.

2 Philosophical Transactions, no. 437, vol. XXXIX, p. 61.

3 Philosophical Transactions, no. 409, vol. XXXVI, p. 125.

4 *Loc. cit.* no. 437, vol. XXXIX, p. 72. He adds (p. 69): "Our house-dogs were also sensible and affected with the earthquake; some of them barking, others howling and making strange and unusual noises."

5 Coffin's History of Newbury, p. 198.

Mr. Henry Sewall, of Newbury, wrote to his kinsman, Judge Samuel Sewall, of Boston, the following letter:[1]

NEWBURY, *November* 21, 1727.

"Honored sir:

Thro' God's goodness to us we are all well, and have been preserved at the time of the late great and terrible earthquake. We were sitting by the fire and about half after ten at night our house shook and trembled as if it would have fallen to pieces. Being affrighted we ran out of doors, when we found the ground did tremble, and we were in great fear of being swallowed up alive; but God preserved us, and did not suffer it to break out, till it got forty or fifty rods from the house, where it brake the ground in the common near a place called Spring island, and there is from sixteen to twenty loads of fine sand thrown out where the ground broke, and several days after the water boiled out like a spring, but is now dry, and the ground closed up again. I have sent some of the sand that you may see it. Our house kept shaking about three minutes."

It is said that several springs of water, and wells that were never known to be dry or frozen, were sunk far down into the earth; and while some were dried up, others had their temperature so altered as to freeze in moderate weather. Some had their water improved, but others were made permanently bad. Some firm land became quagmire, and marshes were dried up. Several phenomena were observed a few days previous to this earthquake, of a nature often observed preceding earthquakes in other countries, especially in Campania. One observer, the Rev. Mr. Allin, of Brookline, says: "Three days before the earthquake there was perceived an ill-stinking smell in the water of several wells. Not thinking of the proper cause, some searched their wells, but found nothing that might thus infect them. The scent was so strong and offensive that for about eight or ten days they entirely omitted using it. In the deepest of these wells, which was about thirty-six feet, the water was turned to a brimstone color, but had nothing of the smell, and was thick like puddle water."

Mr. Dudley, in the account already referred to, says:[2] "A neighbor of mine that had a well thirty-six feet deep, about three days before the earthquake, was surprised to find his water, that used to be very sweet and limpid, stink to that degree that they could make no use of it, nor scarce bear the house when it was brought in; and imagining that some carrion was got into the well, he searched the bottom, but found it clear and good, though the color of the water was turned wheyish, or pale. In about seven days after the earthquake the water began to mend; and in three days more it returned to its former sweetness and color." Several wells dried up just before the earthquake, and were afterwards full again.

The extent of this shock seems to have been from the Kennebeck to the Delaware, although in both of these places the shock was slight. It was felt by vessels at sea off the coast, and also at the extreme western settlements, but its true extent northwest and southeast we have no means of knowing. In "Smith's Journal" it is mentioned as a noteworthy consequence of this uncommon alarm, that a revival of religion took place; "forty out of one hundred and twenty-four" were the fruits of it in Rev. Mr. Emerson's parish in Portsmouth, which was in the most disturbed district.

Several shocks were felt in northern New England for some months after this, but they were slight and of short duration. It will be remembered that on the eighteenth of

[1] Coffin's History of Newbury, p. 198.

[2] Philosophical Transactions, no. 437, vol. XXXIX, p. 72.

November, the city of Tabriz, in Persia, was destroyed by an earthquake, and seventy-seven thousand people perished.[1]

The Rev. Matthias Plant, the minister at Newbury, kept a record of the shocks felt from 1727 to 1741, and from this church record wrote an account to England, which was published,[2] and the essential part is here reprinted. The dates are all in old style:

October 29, 1727, being the Lord's-Day, about forty minutes past ten the same evening, there came a great rumbling noise; but before the noise was heard, or shock perceived, our bricks upon the hearth rose up about three quarters of a foot; and seemed to fall down and loll the other way, which was in half a minute attended with the noise or burst. The tops of our chimneys, stone fences were thrown down; and in some places (in the lower grounds, about three miles from my house) the earth opened and threw out some hundred loads of earth of a different color from that near the surface, something darker than your white marl in England. . . . It continued roaring, bursting and shocking our houses all that night. Though the first was much the loudest and most terrible, yet eight more that came that night were loud, and roared like a cannon at a distance. It continued roaring and bursting twelve times in a day and night, until Thursday in the said week, and then was not so frequent; but upon Friday in the evening, and about midnight, and about break of day upon Saturday, three very loud roarings; we had the roaring noise upon Saturday, Sunday, Monday, about ten in the morning, although much abated in the noise.

November 7 being Tuesday, about eleven it roared very loud, and gave our houses a great shock; and continued shocking from three times to six every day and night, until the twelfth of November, when it was heard twice in one hour in the afternoon, from $3^h\ 30'$ to $4^h\ 30'$.

November 13. Two hours before daybreak the roaring was loud, and shook the houses. Upon Wednesday following, $2^h\ 30'$ in the afternoon, there was a roaring, but not so loud. The noise and shocks continued five, six, to ten times a week, until the seventeenth of December following; and then about half an hour past ten in the evening, it roared very loud and shook our houses very much; another shock the next morning about four o'clock, much abated.

January 3, 1727 28. About nine at night, an easy shock.

January 6. There were five shocks attended with the roaring, from about nine at night to four on Sunday morning; and some people told me, that lived in the low grounds, that for the space of about half an hour it continually kept roaring every half minute or minute.

Wednesday, January 24. About half an hour after nine at night it roared exceedingly loud, and was followed in half a minute with roaring much abated in the noise.

January 28, $6^h\ 30'$ A.M., another easy shock, and another about ten the same morning, easy. On the same night, about 1^h A.M., a loud roaring and shock.

January 29. I heard it twice, though easy, that day.

January 30. About two in the afternoon, there was a very great roaring, equal to any but the first for terror; it shook our houses so as that many people were afraid of their falling down; pewter, etc., was shook off our dressers; . . . . the lead windows in the church rattled to such a degree, as that I thought they would all be broke. And there was another shock the same day, about an hour and half after, though much abated.

February 21. About half an hour past twelve, A.M., a considerable loud roaring with a shock.

February 29. Such another.

March 17. About three in the morning an easy shock.

March 19. At $1^h\ 40'$ P.M., a small noise; at nine the same night a small noise with a shock.

April 28, 1728. At 5^h P.M., a small noise but perceivable.

May 12. About $9^h\ 40'$ a long and loud roaring, and shook the houses.

May 17. About 8^h P.M., a long and loud roaring shook our houses.

May 22. Several small roarings in the morning; but about ten o'clock the same morning, long and loud, and shook our houses.

June 6 and 8. About three o'clock in each morning, a long and loud roaring.

[1] At Salem, Nov. 4, a meeting was held in the house of the first parish on account of the "terrible earthquake." Many attended. Mr. Fisk preached from I Peter, IV, 17, 18. Felt's Annals of Salem, p. 385. A fast was appointed on the 21st of December on the same account. *Ibid*, p. 386.

[2] Philosophical Transactions, no. 462, vol. XLII, p. 33.

June 11. Nine in the morning a small noise.

July 3. About two in the morning.

July 23. About break of day, very loud and long; shook our houses. Besides these times I have mentioned, it has been often heard by me, but the noise was small, so forbore to set them down.

March 19, 1728–9. Betwixt two and three P.M., it was loud and long, shook our houses, being repeated twice in an instant; and this was the longest and loudest roaring, and the greatest shock that I ever heard, the first excepted, and that upon the thirtieth of January. We had several small shocks in this interim.

September 8, 1729. About 3^h 30′ [P.M.?] it was loud and long.

September 29. About 4^h 30′ P.M., loud and long.

October 29. I heard it twice this night. One of the times was about the same time of night the first shock was [10^h 40′ A.M.].

November 14. About eight in the morning loud and long; attended with two bursts like unto two sudden claps of thunder; shook our houses.

November 27. About eight in the evening a very great roaring and a great shock. It was heard at Ipswich, about fourteen miles distant.

February 8, 1729–30. About eight in the evening a small shock, about midnight loud and long, and gave our houses a great shock.

February 26. About 1^h 45′ A.M., the noise was repeated twice in one minute; the first was loud and long, and shook our houses equal to any but the first shock; the second noise was low and seemingly at a distance.

April 12, 1730. About eight in the evening a very loud and long noise, and a great shock.

July 28. About 9^h A.M., a sudden and loud roaring, and shock.

August 15. About 8^h A.M., a shock of the earthquake, twice repeated in a moment of time.

November 6. It was loud and long, and gave my house a jar.

November 14. About 9^h A.M., a small noise and rumbling; no shock.

November 25. About 8^h 20′ P.M., a loud and long roaring, and gave my house a considerable shock.

December 6. About 10^h 45′ P.M., it was loud and roared long, and made our houses jar.

December 11. About 6^h 45′ P. M., there was a small burst, but shaked my house.

December 12. About 10^h 30′ P.M., the earthquake did very much shake our houses, without any noise or roaring, more than ever before, the first time excepted. It was felt at *Boston*, forty miles, at *Piscataqua*, twenty-two miles, almost equal to what it was with us.

January 7, 1730–1. About seven at night it was loud and long, shook our houses.

January 11. About midnight loud and long, shook our houses.

March 7. About five in the evening we heard the noise, but no shock.

May 28, 1731. About nine in the morning I heard the noise of the earthquake very distinctly, but could not perceive that it shook.

July 5. About sunrise it was loud and long, shook our houses.

August 21. Nine o'clock in the evening the noise was small and short.

October 1. About eleven at night loud and long, shook our houses.

February 7, 1731–2. About seven at night a great shock, shook our houses.

September 5, 1732. About noon we had a severe shock, which was perceived at *Boston* and *Piscataqua*, but attended with little or no noise. The same earthquake was heard at Montreal, in Canada, at the same time and about the same hour of the day, and did damage to one hundred and eighty-five houses, killed seven persons, and hurt five others; and it was heard there several times afterwards, only in the night, as the newspapers give us this account. [See below for the extent of this shock.]

December 30. In the morning we had a shock, and it had been heard by some people several times within three weeks before.

March 1. A loud and long noise of it.

October 19, 1733. A loud and long noise about midnight.

January 16, 1733–4. About 10^h 20′ P.M., a loud and long roaring.

June 29, 1734. About 3^h 15′ P.M., there was somewhat of a noise of it.

October 9. About 10^h 20′ A.M., a small shock.

November 11 or 12, for it was about midnight, we had the loudest noise and greatest shock, except the first; it was long, very awful and terrible.

November 16. About six in the morning there was a small shock.

February 2, 1735–6. About a quarter of an hour before six in the evening there was a pretty loud noise and shock.

March 21. About half an hour past ten in the morning it was somewhat loud.

July 13, 1736. About 9^h 45′ A.M., the noise of it was loud.

October 1. About 1^h 30′ A.M., it was long and loud, and a great shock twice repeated in an instant.

November 12. About two in the morning there was a shock with the noise, and about six the same morning, it was something louder.

February 6, 1736–7. About 4^h 15′ P.M., we had a considerable shock.

September 9, 1737. About 10^h 20′ A.M., it was very loud and long, and shook our houses very much.

December 7. A little before eleven in the night the ground shook very much, but [we] heard no noise. Upon the same seventh of December, at *New York*, they had three severe shocks of an earthquake in the night; it threw down there some chimneys, and made the bells to toll so as to be heard. At the same time the said shock and noise was felt and heard in many other places.

August 2, 1739.[1] We had a great shock; it made my house shake much, and the windows jar. It was about half an hour past two in the morning; I think I never heard but two other louder or longer, or greater.

December 14, 1740. About 6^h 35′ A.M., there was heard a pretty loud noise of the earthquake.

January 18, 1740–1. About 4^h A.M., there was heard the noise of the earthquake.

January 25, 1740–1. About ten minutes before four in the afternoon, there was a shock of the earthquake with a loud rumbling noise. This is the last that has been heard (and I pray God I may never hear any more such, and so long). I have omitted to set down some that were small, or such as I did not hear myself; I was very exact to the time, so that what account I have sent you is most certainly true. * * * And although the first night was the most terrible, as the surprise was sudden; yet there never happened one shock amongst us but what occasioned some alteration at that time in every person's countenance or constitution; and which way soever any person's face happened to be, that way the noise of the earthquake appeared to him. * * * These frequent repetitions of the roaring and shocks of the earthquake were upon Merrimack River, and seldom extended above seven or eight miles distance from, or twenty or thirty up the said river, those instances only excepted which I have mentioned in the relation; and the first shock of it was greater with us than anywhere else in New England; and the tops of chimneys and stone fences were thrown down only in these parts.[2]

It is said that on the Tuesday preceding September 15, 1728, a shock was felt at Newbury, at four o'clock A.M., preceded by a noise like thunder,[3] but Mr. Plant does not mention it.

January 30, 1728, at 2^h P.M. a distinct shock was felt at Boston, but no damage 1728.
was done. From November 9, 1727 to August 2, 1728, there were several slight shocks felt in New England.

September 15, 1732. A violent earthquake was felt in Canada, which did con- 1732.
siderable damage at Montreal, as stated in the preceding list. It came at eleven o'clock A.M., and was attended with a rumbling noise. A clock was stopped at Annapolis, Maryland, although the shock was slightly felt at Boston.[4] In June, of the next year, on the fourteenth, according to some authorities, it is said a shock was felt at Annapolis, but there is no certainty that it took place.

On *February* 16, 1737, at 4^h 30′ P.M., shocks were felt at Boston. *December* 1737.
17, shortly before eleven o'clock at night, shocks were felt at New York (three during the night) and Boston, severe enough to throw down several chimneys in the former city, as described by Mr. Plant. In *October* or *November* of the same year a very

[1] Reverend Samuel Phillips, of Andover, notes in an almanac, under this date; "The night following was an earthquake yᵉ noise long and loud." Felt's Annals of Salem.

[2] This letter was read February 21, 1742.

[3] Philosophical Transactions, vol. XXXVI, p. 127.

[4] Philosophical Transactions, no. 429, vol. XXXVIII, p. 120.

slight shock was felt in Boston,[1] but it is only referred to as happening about seventeen years before the great earthquake of 1755.

1741. *December* 6, 1741, a small earthquake was felt at Boston, Dedham, Walpole, and other towns about eight o'clock in the morning.[2]

On Sunday, *June* 13, 1741, at 10^h 35′ A.M., a very noisy earthquake took place, although the shock was not very great. The day was bright and hot, and the barometer fell slightly (two lines) in the morning. There had been no rain since the twenty-third of May, and the whole month was dry and hot. Much lightning was observed during the latter part of the month. At the time of the earthquake the barometer, as observed by Professor Winthrop, stood at 29.94.[3]

1744. On *May* 16, 1744, a considerable vibration felt at Quebec, Canada. *June* 3, a slight shock at Cambridge, Massachusetts. *December* 23, a small earthquake was felt about Newbury at noon.[4]

1746. *February* 2, 1746, a shock was felt by some at Boston, between nine and ten in the evening. A very remarkable aurora borealis was observed a month later.[5]

1755. The year of the great Lisbon earthquake was long remembered in New England, and careful accounts were prepared at the time by Professor John Winthrop, of Cambridge, and published both in this country and in England.[6] The shock which had destroyed the city of Lisbon, with so many of her inhabitants, was felt from Iceland on the north to Morocco on the south, from Bohemia to the West Indies. After an interval of only eighteen days, and during this time slight shocks had been felt in Europe, as if the vibration of the earth's crust still continued from the first great impulse, New England and the neighboring parts of America were shaken. On Tuesday, *November* 18, 1755, at 4^h 11′ 35″,[7] after a perfectly calm night, with the moon, which was near (thirty-six hours) the full, shining brightly, the shock came. Like the other earthquakes of New England, this began with a roaring noise from the northwest, like distant thunder. A man who was on the road at the time, heard the noise and recognized its nature as it grew louder, and in about a minute he felt the shock, which resembled a long rolling sea; and the swell was so great that he was obliged to run and catch hold of something to prevent being thrown down. The tops of two trees near him, one twenty-five and the other thirty feet high, waved, he thought, ten feet. This motion was repeated, and then came a smaller one, and it was supposed that the shock was passed. "But instantly," Winthrop says, "without a moment's intermission, the shock came on with redoubled noise and violence, though the species of it was altered to a tremor, or quick horizontal vibratory motion, with sudden jerks and wrenches. The bed on which I lay was now tossed from side to side; the whole house was prodigiously agitated; the windows rattled, the beams cracked, as if all would presently be shaken to pieces. When this had continued about two minutes it began to abate, and gradually kept decreasing, as if it would soon be over; however, before it had quite ceased, there was a little revival of the trembling and noise, though no ways comparable to what had been before, but this presently decreased, till all, by degrees, became still

[1] Philosophical Transactions, vol. XLIX (pt. I), p. 443.

[2] Silliman's Journal, vol. XL, p. 204.

[3] Philosophical Transactions, vol. L (pt. I), p. 14.

[4] Silliman's Journal, vol. XL. p. 205.

[5] *Loc. cit.*

[6] Philosophical Transactions, vol. L, (pt. I, 1757), p. 1, *et seq.*

[7] Prof. Winthrop had regulated both his clock and watch the previous noon, and a tall glass tube that he had enclosed in the clock case for safety was thrown against the pendulum at the first shock, stopping the clock.

and quiet. Thus ended this great shock. It was followed by another about an hour and a quarter after, viz., at 5^h 29′. This, though comparatively small, was very generally perceived, both as to its noise and trembling, by those who were awake. On the Saturday evening following (*November* 22), at twenty-seven minutes after eight, there was a third, more considerable than the second, but not to be compared with the first. And on Friday, *December* 19, in the evening exactly at ten o'clock, there was a fourth shock, much smaller than either of the former, though like them, preceded by the peculiar noise of an earthquake. The whole lasted but a few seconds; but the jarring was great enough to cause the window shutters and door of the room in which I then was, to clatter. The sky was perfectly clear. * * * These four are the only shocks that I have been sensible of, from the eighteenth of November last, to this date (*January* 10, 1756); though more are said to have been felt in other parts of the country to the northward of us." On the day of the first shock, nine hours after it was felt at Cambridge, or about two o'clock in the afternoon, the sea withdrew from the harbor of St. Martin's in the West Indies, leaving vessels dry, and fish on banks where the depth of water was usually three or four fathoms. It would seem from this, and from the observation of the direction of the sound, that the earthquake vibrated from northwest to southeast, and of course its secondary impulses were transverse to this primary line. As it moved much slower than sound, as was shown by the fact that it was heard nearly a minute before the motion was felt, it would not be unreasonable to suppose that as sound would require two hours and a quarter to go such a distance, the earthquake wave impeded by ocean currents, may have required nine hours to send its secondary waves to the harbor of St. Martin's.

How far did the shock extend? Professor Winthrop says:[1] "By the best information that I can procure, the limit toward the southwest was Chesapeake Bay, in Maryland, the shock having been felt on the eastern side of that bay and not on the western. For the other limit towards the northeast, we are informed that the earthquake was felt at Annapolis Royal, in Nova Scotia, though in a much less degree than with us. It shook off a few bricks from the tops of some chimneys, but was not perceived by vessels on the water." It was not felt north of Halifax, but the army at Lake George perceived a slight trembling; and in the Atlantic, seventy leagues to the east of Cape Ann, the people on board a vessel supposed they had run aground, so violent was the shock, but their lead showed fifty fathoms of water. If we consider the tidal wave at the West Indies a result as well as a consequent of this New England shock, we shall have a line nearly nineteen hundred miles long, and the shortest diameter of the shaken region would be almost five hundred miles, but the intensity of vibration rapidly diminished away from the central line.

If all previously recorded earthquakes in New England were unimportant, and sent, as Morton says, for "gentle warnings unto us to shake us out of our earthly-mindedness, spiritual security and other sins, lest the Lord do come against us with judgment of this kind in the sorest and worst sort of them," that of 1755 was one of great severity. In Boston, the damage done was considerable, as is shown by Professor Winthrop.[2] "Besides the throwing down of glass, pewter, and other movables in the houses, many chimneys

[1] *Loc. cit.* p. 9.

[2] *Loc. cit.* p. 11.

were levelled with the roofs of the houses, and many more shattered and thrown down in part. Some were broken off several feet below the top, and, by the suddenness and violence of the jerks, canted horizontally an inch or two over, so as to stand very dangerously. Some others were twisted or turned round in part. The roofs of some houses were quite broken in by the fall of chimneys; and the gable ends of some brick buildings thrown down, and many were cracked. The vane upon the public market house was thrown down; the wooden spindle which supported it, about five inches in diameter, and which had stood the most violent gusts of wind, being snapped off. A new vane upon one of the churches was bent at its spindle, two or three points of the compass; and another at Springfield was bent to a right angle. A distiller's cistern, made of plank, almost new, and very strong put together, was burst to pieces by the agitation of the liquor in it; which was thrown out with such force as to break down one whole side of the shed that defended the cistern from the weather." Another account says "that in some places, especially on the low, loose ground made by encroachments on the harbor, the streets are almost covered with the bricks that have fallen." [1]

All through the country stone fences were thrown down, but especially on a line extending from Montreal to Boston. New springs were opened and old ones dried up. At Pembroke, Scituate and Lancaster, in Massachusetts, chasms opened in the earth; and at Pembroke "there were four or five of them, out of some of which water issued, and many cart loads of a fine, whitish and compressible sand were spewed." In the harbor the shock was felt by those in vessels as if they were beating upon the bottom; and immediately after the earthquake large numbers of fish came to the surface, some dead and others dying. This was doubtless due to the unusual disengagement of carburetted and sulphuretted gases from the bottom, by the shock. Several slight shocks were felt for several months after this all over the country.

The motion was much greater in the upper parts of a house than in the lower. A key was thrown from a shelf in a southwest direction, although it could have fallen any other way except southeast. Some bricks which fell from the top of a chimney, a height of thirty-two feet, were found thirty feet from the base of a perpendicular. The barometer and thermometer underwent no change during the time of the earthquake.

Mr. John Hyde says: [2] "Many chimneys, I conjecture (from observation) not much less than an hundred, are levelled with the roofs of the houses; many more, I imagine not fewer than twelve or fifteen hundred, are shattered and thrown down in part."

November 21 and *December* 19 slight shocks at Boston.

1756. *January* 2, 1756, a shock was felt in Boston, according to Keferstein.[3]

November 16, 1756, about four o'clock in the morning a small earthquake, which seemed not to last above two seconds. All I perceived was the rattling of the window shutters by my bed's head. The sky was covered. Little or no wind. The weather moderate. It was more sensibly perceived in other towns" [than Cambridge].[4] *December* 4, 10^h P. M., a slight shock.[5]

1757. *July* 8, 1757, at 2^h 15′ P. M., a considerable shaking was felt at Boston, but it was of short duration.[6]

[1] Philosophical Transactions, vol. XLIX, (pt. I), p. 441.

[2] *Loc. cit.*

[3] Mallet's Catalogue.

[4] Observations of Professor Winthrop in Silliman's Journal, vol. XL, p. 206.

[5] *Loc. cit.*

[6] *Loc. cit.*

April 24, 1758, 9^h 30′ P.M., a trembling lasting thirty seconds and preceded by subterranean noises which increased by degrees, was felt at Annapolis, Maryland, and more feebly in Pennsylvania.[1]

February 2, 1758, a slight shock at Boston. The date 1759 is given in the 1758.
Annual Register, quoted by Mallet.[2]

February 3, 1760, slight in New England.[3] 1760.

November 9, at Boston a slight tremor.[4] More severe in the neighborhood.

February, at Boston, no mensual date given.[5] 1761.

March 12 and 16,[6] in New England, especially at Boston, more violent on the former date. "Salem, March 12. We were, last night, about quarter past two o'clock, roused out of our beds by an astonishing earthquake, much such as that five years ago, only that was a more terrible jar and this was undulating."[7] The later date is perhaps a mistake. Professor Williams does not mention it, but describes the earthquake of the 12th as slight, commencing at 2^h 30′ A.M., with a slight shock, followed after a slight pause by another more violent. The weather was moderate, perfectly calm, and a whitish fog covered the horizon all around. It was felt in all the neighboring States.[8]

November 1, 8^h P.M., a shock was felt through Massachusetts and in New Hampshire. It was preceded by the usual rumbling noise, and its course was from northwest to southeast.[9]

October 30, 1763, 4^h 15′ P.M., a shock was felt in Philadelphia which interrupted services in the churches, but did no damage. Our only authority for this, however, is a newspaper report.[10]

February 2, 1766. In Massachusetts and Rhode Island, and other parts of New 1766.
England, accompanied by a remarkable meteor.[11]

June 14, in Essex County, Massachusetts.

August 25, at Newport, Rhode Island, a violent shock lasting twenty-five minutes.

December 17, 6^h 48′ at Portsmouth, New Hampshire, a violent shock.[12] An earthquake reported on February 2, 1776, did not occur.

November 29, 1783, about 10^h 50′ P.M., an earthquake was felt from New 1783.
Hampshire to Pennsylvania. It was slight, and at Boston and in New England generally, only one shock was felt, and that from north to south and continuing about one minute. At New York three shocks were felt about 9^h, 11^h P.M., and 2^h A.M. At Philadelphia, one about 9^h P.M., and another about 2^h A.M.[13]

January 2, 1785, 7^h 15′ A.M., a shock was felt at Cambridge, Massachusetts, 1785.
and at the same time at Baltimore, Maryland.[14]

November 29, 1786, 4^h P.M., at Cambridge.[15] 1786.

February 25, 1787, 1^h A.M., again at Cambridge.[16] 1787.

1 Collection Académique, t. VI, p. 688.

2 Doddesley's Annual Register, vol. II. p. 88.

3 Annual Register, vol. III, p. 92.

4 Gazette de France, Jan. 31, 1761.

5 Journal Historique, Juillet, 1761, p. 65.

6 Annual Register, vol. IV, p. 117.

7 Smith's Journal quoted in Felt's Annals of Salem, p. 457.

8 Memoirs of the American Academy, vol. I, p. 278.

9 *Loc. cit.* p. 279.

10 Gazette de France, 9 Janvier, 1764.

11 Silliman's Journal, vol. XXXIX, p. 336.

12 Annual Register, vol. X, p. 52. The Gazette de France, 6 Mars, 1767, gives the date as 13, and the time 6^h 40′ P.M.

13 Professor Williams, *loc. cit.* p. 279. The Gazette de Leyde, Jan. 23, 1784, gives the time of the shocks at New York as 10^h 30′ P.M., and 2^h 30′ A.M.

14 Éphémeris de Mannheim, 1785, p. 582. Von Hoff, Geschichte der Veränderungen, t. II, s. 541, merely refers to it

15 *Loc. cit.* p. 590.

16 *Loc. cit.* 1787, p. 350.

1791. The region around East Haddam on the Connecticut River, a few miles below Middletown, has been the scene of a series of local disturbances which have been noticed since the country was settled, and are referred to by Indian tradition and their name of the place, *Morehemoodus*, or place of noises.[1] The first shock of which the time is recorded was on *May* 16, 1791, at eight o'clock in the morning, when it began by two very heavy shocks in quick succession. The first was more violent. Stone walls were shaken down, chimneys were untopped, latched doors thrown open, and a fissure in the ground several rods long supposed to be then opened as it was discovered soon after. Thirty lighter shocks succeeded in a short time, and more than a hundred were counted during the night. At Killingworth, twenty miles distant, "a Captain Benedict who was walking the deck of his vessel, then lying in the harbor of that place, observed the fish to leap out of water in every direction as far as his eye could reach." The atmosphere was clear, and the very bright moon almost full. On the night of the seventeenth, six more shocks were felt. The weather continued clear and warm.[2]

May 18, 1791, about ten o'clock, P.M., a shock was felt from Boston to New York. A few minutes after came another lesser shock, perceptible at a distance of seventy miles from East Haddam.[3] There the tremor of the earth and the noise in the atmosphere were great. Chimneys and stone fences were thrown down. During the night there was a succession of local shocks to the number of twenty or thirty. Stones of several tons weight were removed from their places, clefts opened in the soil and in the rocks. In Middle Haddam the shock was quite severe, and the direction seemed to be nearly from west to east. It is probable that the earthquake felt at Philadelphia and New York at the same hour, was identical, and not on the sixteenth as reported.[4]

In *December*, an earthquake was felt at St. Paul's Bay, on the St. Lawrence, in Canada, about sixty miles northeast of Quebec. Walls were cracked and stones fell from the houses.[5]

1792. *August* 28, 1792, another earthquake was felt at East Haddam. The forenoon was rainy with an easterly wind which changed in the afternoon to southwesterly. Warm and somewhat squally. Shock at ten o'clock in the evening.[6] *October* 24, at one o'clock in the morning three shocks were felt. The weather was very pleasant.

1793. *January* 11, 1793, at eight o'clock in the morning, another shock of the East Haddam series. Weather warm and pleasant. *July* 6, another at six o'clock in the morning. Weather very warm and damp; rain, with thunder, in the afternoon.

1794. *March* 6, 1794, at two o'clock in the afternoon, there were two, and another at eleven in the evening. Atmosphere clear in the morning, but damp and hazy in

[1] In a letter from Roger Williams to John Winthrop, dated at Providence, probably June 1638, after referring to the earthquake of that year, the writer continues: "The younger natiues are ignorant of the like: but the ellder informe me that this is the 5th within these 4 score yeare, in the land: the first about 3 score & 10 yeare since: the second some 3 score & 4 yeare since, the third some 54 yeare since, the 4th some 46 since: & they allwayes observed either plague, or pox, or some other epidemicall disease followed; 3, 4, or 5 yeare after the Earthquake (or Naunaumemoauke) as they speake." Massachusetts Historical Collections, (4th ser.) vol. IV, p. 229. Perhaps these traditions referred to earthquakes from this same eastern Connecticut centre.

[2] Silliman's Journal, vol. XXXIX, p. 338.

[3] Trumbull's History of Connecticut, vol. II, p. 92.

[4] Hamburg Corresp. nr. 128; Moniteur, 23 Août 1791, according to Mallet.

[5] Transactions Royal Geological Society (London), 2d vol. V, p. 97, note to Baddeley's Memoir.

[6] Silliman's Journal, *loc. cit.* Mallet confounds this with the next.

the afternoon. It is reported that a shock was felt in Canada in 1796, "a little before March 6," and some rocks at Niagara Falls were dislodged. Keferstein mentions this, but the fact seems doubtful.[1]

Von Hoff mentions a shock felt at Philadelphia, March 17, 1800, and a severe 1800.
shock is said to have occurred at the same place November 29 of the same year.[2] On *December* 25, a severe shock was felt at Newport, Boston, Concord, and elsewhere.[3] In November, between the evening of the eleventh and morning of the twelfth, a vibratory shock was felt.[4] *March* 1, 1801, an earthquake is reported.[5] August 23, 1801.
1802, a severe shock, attended with a noise like the rattling of a carriage on pavement, was felt at Richmond, in Virginia. (Moniteur, 26 Vendémiaire, an 11.) No other authority has been found, and these letters of occasional correspondents are to be received with great caution.

August 11, 1805, at seven o'clock in the evening, two slight shocks were felt at 1805.
the Haddam locality. Wind southwest in the forenoon, and a thunder storm about four, P.M. Another was felt on *December* 30, at six o'clock in the morning. The atmosphere was moist.[6] At Weston, in Connecticut, a remarkable meteor exploded in December, 1807, and some have referred the concussion produced to an earthquake.[7]

The Haddam earthquakes were described by the Reverend Mr. Hosmer, of that town, in a letter to Reverend Mr. Prince, of Boston, dated August 13, 1729. Portions of his account are here given:—"As to the earthquakes, I have something considerable and awful to tell you. Earthquakes have been here, (and nowhere but in this precinct, as can be discovered; that is, they seem to have their centre, rise and origin among us), as has been observed for more than thirty years. I have been informed that in this place, before the English settlements, there were great numbers of Indian inhabitants, and that it was a place of extraordinary *Indian powwows*; or in short, that it was a place where the Indians drove a prodigious trade at worshipping the devil."

"Now whether there be anything diabolical in these things, I know not; but this I know, that God Almighty is to be seen and trembled at, in what has been often heard among us. Whether it be fire or air distressed in the subterraneous caverns of the earth, cannot be known; for there is no eruption, no explosion perceptible, but by sounds and tremors, which sometimes are very fearful and dreadful. I have myself heard eight or ten sounds successively, and imitating small arms, in the space of five minutes. I have, I suppose, heard several hundreds of them within twenty years; some more, some less terrible. Sometimes we have heard them almost every day, and great numbers of them in the space of a year. Oftentimes I have observed them to be coming down from the north, imitating slow thunder, until the sound came near, or right under, and then there seemed to be a breaking, like the noise of a cannon shot, or severe thunder, which shakes the houses and all that is in them. They have, in a manner, closed since the great earthquake. As I remember, there have been but two known since that time, and those but moderate."[8] Dr. Trumbull, in his history from which the above is quoted, writing about the beginning of the present century, says: "A worthy gentleman, about six years since,

[1] Bibliothèque Britannique, t. II, p. 86.
[2] Hamburg Correspondence, 1801, nr. 15.
[3] Moniteur, 24 Ventose an 9.
[4] Hamb. Correspond. nr. 25, 1802.
[5] Felt's Annals of Salem, II, p. 143.
[6] Silliman's Journal, vol. XXXIX, p. 339.
[7] *Loc. cit.* p. 336.
[8] Trumbull's History of Connecticut, vol. II, p. 92.

gave the following account of them." "The awful noises of which Mr. Hosmer gave an account in his historical minutes, continue to the present time. The effects they produce are various as the intermediate degrees between the roar of a cannon and the noise of a pistol. The concussions of the earth, made at the same time, are as much diversified as the sounds in the air. The shock they give to a dwelling house, is the same as the falling of logs on the floor. The smaller shocks produced no emotions of terror or fear in the minds of the inhabitants. They are spoken of as usual occurrences, and are called 'Moodus noises.' But when they are so violent as to be heard in the adjacent towns, they are called earthquakes. During my residence here, which has been almost thirty-six years, I have invariably observed, after some of the most violent of these shocks, that an account has been published in the newspapers of a small shock of an earthquake at New London and Hartford. Nor do I believe, in all that period, there has been an account published of an earthquake in Connecticut, which was not far more violent here than in any other place." Although these noises still continue, as will be seen by the list, yet they are now infrequent. No explanation of their usually local character has been given, and the Moodus Hill, or Mount Tom, seems never to have been accurately described by any one acquainted with volcanic formations. It will be noticed, however, that the geological structure of this region is much disturbed.

1810. *November* 9, 1810, at 9^h 15′ P.M., at Exeter, New Hampshire, an earthquake was felt which was accompanied by a very unusual noise. The account given by Judge Samuel Tenney[1] is quite clear and distinct. He was sitting by the fireside when he heard a "very heavy and singular noise" directly under his feet; this was immediately followed by a tremendous report in the atmosphere, which did not, however, shake the house. "It was instantly succeeded by the sound usually attending an earthquake," whatever this may be, "continuing with some little variation of intensity for some forty or fifty seconds," and the vibrations which were felt at the same time were steady and not violent. No damage was done, although animals were frightened. The explosion was heard at Conway, seventy or eighty miles north of Exeter. The shock was most violent between Haverhill and Portsmouth, and its course was northwest and southeast. It was felt on the water, and a vessel running into Portsmouth harbor seemed to those on board to strike bottom. Several persons in different towns who were awake, felt a second shock towards morning.

The Moniteur newspaper contains[2] a letter from Boston, dated November 14, which states the time at 9^h 3′ P.M. The shock at Portsmouth lasted one or two minutes; windows were broken. At Kennebunk there were several shocks during twenty seconds. At Portland the vibration was very slight; the air was very calm until a moment before the shock, when a violent wind arose suddenly.

The earthquakes which shook the Valley of the Mississippi from December 16, 1811, to 1813, were slightly felt to the east of the Alleghanies, and not at all in New England; but during the continuance of this series another of the local disturbances was felt at East
1812. Haddam, Connecticut. On *February* 9, 1812, at 9^h A.M., two slight rumblings were felt. The weather was clear. *July* 5, at 8^h A.M., another of the Haddam shocks. Atmosphere filled with mist and rain.

[1] Memoirs American Academy, vol. III, p. 346. [2] Janvier 18, 1811.

December 28, 1813, at 4^h P.M., during wet weather, another rumbling was heard at East Haddam.[1] 1813.

September 9, 1816, a severe shock was felt at Montreal, and on the sixteenth of the same month a second shock of less violence than the former lasted thirty seconds. These were hardly felt in central New England.[2] 1816.

October 5, an earthquake is reported. Walls were thrown down at Woburn, Massachusetts.[3] 1817.

October 11, 1818, strong shocks were felt along the base of the mountains to the north of Quebec. (Qu. Watckish Mts.) The windows and furniture of the houses were shaken.[4] 1818.

About the middle of *November*, 1819, a slight shock was felt at Montreal, which was followed by a tempest in which rain fell of an inky blackness.[5] 1819.

At the end of *February*, 1821, a slight shock was felt at Quebec, but not noticed in New England.[6] In 1823, May 30, the water rose nine feet in Lake Erie; a slight shock.[7] 1821.

July 9, 1824, a severe shock was felt at New Brunswick, accompanied by a noise like the discharge of cannon.[8] 1824.

October 15, 1826, a violent earthquake was felt at Savannah, in Georgia.

August 6, 1827, at 10^h P.M., a slight shock was felt in Indiana. And on the twenty-third of the same month a shock was felt at New London, Connecticut, accompanied by a noise like the rolling of a heavy wagon, the noise increasing for three or four seconds and then decreasing for an equal time.[9] 1827.

August 20, 1828, a light shock was felt in some parts of Canada. February 24, 1828, a violent shock is reported at Washington and Baltimore; and on March 9, between 10^h and 11^h P.M., two severe shocks were felt, lasting in all 30″.[10] 1828.

In *January*, 1829, at the beginning of the month a slight shock is reported at Portsmouth, New Hampshire.[11] 1829.

July 14, 1831, walls and chimneys were thrown down at Murray Bay, Canada.[12] The next year a slight shock was felt at Nova Scotia. 1831.

The shocks were repeated at Murray Bay in March and April.[13] 1833.

April 12, 1837, an earthquake occurred at Hartford, Connecticut, slight, but enough to jar all loose articles, and swing a pendant lamp. In one house a bell rang, and some people ran out of their houses, thinking they were about to fall.[14] 1837.

On Sunday, *August* 9, 1840, an earthquake was distinctly felt in many parts of Connecticut. At Hartford the people rushed from the churches. But in New 1840.

[1] Silliman's Journal, vol. XXXIX, p. 339.

[2] Journal des Débats, Janvier 1, 1817.

[3] Felt's Annals of Salem, vol. II, p. 143.

[4] Annales de Chimie et de Physique, t. XII, p. 426. Quarterly Journal of the Royal Institution, vol. VI, p. 370.

[5] *Ibid*, t. XV, p. 422. *Ibid*, vol. IX, p. 205.

[6] *Ibid*, t. XVIII, p. 415. Archives des Découvertes 1822, p. 190, only repeats the same as preceding reference.

[7] Transactions of the Literary and Philosophical Society, New York, vol. II, p. 1, § 25.

[8] *Ibid*, 1824, p. 213. Annales de Chimie et de Physique, t. XXVII, p. 378.

[9] Columbus, Dec. 1827, s. 197.

[10] Monthly Magazine, August, 1828, p. 202. December 11, 1828, a shock was felt in Georgia.

[11] Preussische Staatszeitung 1829. nr. 62. Von Hoff, Chronik, t. II, p. 315, adds that it occurred in the night.

[12] Transactions of the Society of Quebec, vol. II, pp. 83, 89, 1831.

[13] Transactions of the Geological Society (London), vol. V, p. 98, note. Murray Bay is the centre of frequent disturbances.

[14] Silliman's Journal, vol. XXXII, p. 339.

Haven it was not at all felt in the churches, and only slightly by a few people in their own houses. "At North Milford, six miles west of New Haven, it was not perceived. At Milford, still further west, and at Bridgeport, it was felt and heard distinctly. Hence we hear of it to the north and northeast as very distinct, nine to twenty-five miles from New Haven. It was very perceptible in some parts of Massachusetts — not at all in Westfield. In Worcester County it was severe. In Boston there was nothing of it." Some observers thought the noise proceeded from east to west, others from northeast to southwest; and one who was used to earthquakes, thought that at Chester, in Connecticut, near East Haddam, the rumbling continued half a minute, and its course was from northwest to southeast. At Chester, twenty-five miles east of New Haven, the shock was distinctly noticed. The sound was compared to the roll of thunder, the rumbling of a carriage, and the roar of a chimney on fire. The weather was clear, and the sun shining bright. There seems to be no record of the time of day.[1] *September* 10. A violent shock at Hamilton, Canada, from west to east.

November 11, 1840, a severe shock was felt at Philadelphia, accompanied by a great and unusually sudden swell in the Delaware. On the fourteenth of the same month, there was a noise and shock observed in Philadelphia (not New Haven, as Mallet has it), but the members of the American Philosophical Society could not determine whether it was caused by an earthquake or a meteor.[2]

1841. *January* 25, 1841, several shocks were felt in New York in the morning, lasting from fifteen to twenty seconds in all, with a direction from west to east.[3] During this year a shock was reported in Canada, but it is very doubtful. A large mass of rock fell from a cliff, and was probably the origin of the shocks, as in February, 1796, when a fall of part of the ledge at Niagara Falls caused a tremor which was credited to an earthquake.

1842. *November* 9, 1842, an earthquake at Montreal, Three Rivers, and other parts of Canada, when "the waters of the St. Lawrence were violently agitated."[4]

1845. *October* 26, 1845, a slight shock was felt at New York, and in the western part of New England.

1846. *May* 30, 1848, at 1^h 30′ P.M., a shock was distinctly felt at Newburyport, Salem, and adjacent towns. *July* 10, a series of shocks commenced at Deerfield, New Hampshire, which continued on *September* 12, at sunset; *October* 29, at 9^h P.M.; 31, at night; *December* 2. None of these were severe, and as Deerfield is on the line between Newbury and Montreal, it is remarkable that these tremors were not felt at a greater distance. They were repeated the next year.

1847. *January* 8, 1847, about 3^h P.M., a shock at Grafton Harbor, and a remarkable tide on Lake Ontario. *January* 11, at 11^h 30′ P.M., a shock at Albany, N. Y. The Journal of Commerce, of January 20, reports a slight shock at Lincolnville and Camden, Maine. *February* 2, at Deerfield. On the fourteenth at Meredith Village, New Hampshire, on the nineteenth at Belfast, Maine, and on the twenty-first at Deerfield. All these were light, and very local. *April* 1, at 9^h P.M., at Limington, Maine. *June* 9, a tide was noticed at Lake Winnepiseogee, New Hampshire. *July* 9, in the morning a shock was felt at Glens

[1] Silliman's Journal, vol. XXXIX (2), p. 335. Hartford and New Haven Congregational Observer, August 2, 1840.

[2] Silliman's Journal, vol. XL (2), p. 376.

[3] Comptes Rendus, t. XII, p. 449.

[4] British Association Report. Transactions of Sections, 1845, p. 20. Moniteur Dec. 5, 1842.

Falls. *August* 8, about 10^h A.M., an earthquake was reported at Boston, Dedham, Cape Cod and Nantucket, but not to the north.

The beginning of this year, *January* 1 and *February* 1, shocks are reported in 1848.
Nova Scotia; the first broke the ice on ponds and opened doors, the second occurred at Yarmouth and Sherburne. It is well known that intense cold, as well as intense heat, causes cracking and subterranean rumbling, and it is necessary to guard against mistaking the origin of similar results. These shocks should probably be referred to atmospheric agencies.

May 23, a shock was felt at Montreal, followed the next day by a torrent of rain.

September 9, about 10^h P.M., a shock was reported in Rhode Island, Connecticut, New York, New Jersey and Pennsylvania. The Moniteur of September 29, states that a slight shock had just been felt in the northern United States, and this is doubtless the one intended.

November 6, at 5^h 15′ A.M., a light shock at Grand Island, in the St. Lawrence.

December 11, at 3^h A.M., a tremor at Montreal.

February 4, 1849, at Newport, Rhode Island. 1849.

February 15, at Springfield, Massachusetts, also in St. Lawrence Co., New York.

October 8, in the afternoon, through Middlesex County, Massachusetts.

July 20, 1850, at Portland, Maine, in the afternoon. 1850.

January 3, 1851, at Waterville, Maine. 1851.

January 30, at 5^h P.M., a light shock at St. Andrews, Canada.

January 10, 1852, a shock was noticed at Bedford, Massachusetts, which seems 1852.
to have extended westward to the Connecticut River. The time given in the reports from New Bedford, Providence, Warwick, was 6^h 40′ A.M.

February 11, 5^h 40′ A.M., at St. Martins, Canada, a light shock from the west-northwest. The barometer stood at 29.067; the thermometer at 38.5 F.

April 30, in the afternoon, a shock was felt in the Eastern States, but principally at Washington and Baltimore.

June 30, at Claremont, New Hampshire, and Windsor, Vermont, both on the Connecticut River.

August 1, at Groton, Connecticut.

August 2, about 11^h P.M., at Bathurst, New Brunswick.

August 11, P.M., at Deerfield again.

November 27, 11^h 45′ P.M., an explosion and a dull noise or rumbling was heard at Newburyport, and through the Valley of the Merrimack, at Beverly, Ipswich, Woburn, Topsfield, Groton, Salem, Danvers and Wareham, Massachusetts, and Portsmouth and Exeter, New Hampshire. At the latter place, the shock lasted half a minute, and shook the houses so as to wake people.[1]

March 12, 1853, between two and three o'clock in the morning, a shock was 1853.
noticed at Lowville, New York, which threw down machinery. Its direction was east to west, or the reverse, as observers did not agree.[2] Felt also in Canada.

May 24, at Bytown, Canada.

June 3, two or three shocks at Bridgetown, Nova Scotia.

[1] Silliman's Journal (2), vol. XV, p. 140.

[2] Silliman's Journal (2), vol. XVI, p. 294.

July 17, between 5^h and 6^h A.M., two shocks at Portland, Saco, and other places in Maine.

September 7, 11^h 10′ P.M., at New Bedford and Dartmouth, Massachusetts.

1854. *February* 22–23, 1854, midnight a shock and rumbling, from west to east, was felt and heard at Reading, Massachusetts.

October, a shock at Keene, New Hampshire.

December 4, at 10^h P.M., a shock at Huntington, Canada.

December 10, 12^h 30′ P.M., at Newburyport, Massachusetts, and Exeter and Portsmouth, New Hampshire.

1855. *February* 8, 1855, in Nova Scotia, New Brunswick, and New England, a slight shock. On the nineteenth of the same month a shock in Maine.

1856. *May* 1, 1856, a slight shock at Ottawa, Canada.

December 28, a slight shock at Ottawa, reported by Dawson.[1]

1857. In the Upper Province, Canada, in October, slight.

1858. *May* 10, 1858, at Richmond, Canada.

May 17, P.M., light shock at Richmond. At Sherbrook, about 3^h P.M., the ground moved feebly, with a sound like distant thunder, apparently from the northwest. At Melbourne and Compton the animals seemed much alarmed.

June 30, 10^h 45′ P.M., at New Haven, the tremor lasted more than a minute, accompanied by a sound like a carriage on a bridge, but more sonorous and prolonged; from southwest to northeast. The sky was clear and the air perfectly calm. At Derby the shock was severer than at New Haven; the houses were strongly shaken.[2]

October 8, at 3^h 15′ P.M., a shock was felt in western New York, principally at Buffalo, but also in Canada. The northern end of the line of disturbance seems to have been Port Hope, on Lake Ontario, and the southern, near Warren, Pennsylvania.[3] Eastward it did not pass the Adirondacs, but from its extent into the Montreal region is mentioned in this list. On the eighth of this month a marked shock was felt at St. Louis, and also in Illinois.[4]

1859. A slight shock at Metis, in Canada.[5]

1860. *March* 16, 1860, at 9^h 30′ and at 10^h 15′ P.M., Provincetown, Massachusetts, was visited by two shocks. At Dedham the second shock was felt, attended by a noise like a heavy body falling from the top of a house. It was perceived at Holliston.

October 17, 6^h A.M., an earthquake was felt in Canada, and the northern United States. A number of observations were made, and the following list, prepared by Professor J. W. Dawson, of Montreal, gives a tolerably satisfactory view of the region shaken. The places are arranged in longitudinal order from east to west.[6]

Bic, 6^h A.M. Three shocks at intervals of some seconds, noise continued ten minutes.

Green Island, 6^h A.M.

Rivière du Loup, 6^h A.M. A series of shocks lasting nearly five minutes. A schooner off this place experienced a shock resembling that of striking on a sandbank, and the waters of the Gulf of St. Lawrence were unusually agitated.

[1] Canadian Naturalist and Geologist, vol. I.
[2] Silliman's Journal (2), vol. XXVI, p. 298.
[3] *Ibid*, vol. XXVI, p. 177.
[4] *Ibid*, vol. XXV, p. 136.
[5] Canadian Naturalist and Geologist, vol. V, p. 372.
[6] *Ibid*, vol. V, p. 364.

Rivière Ouelle, 6^h 15′ A.M. Very violent, damaging walls and throwing down chimneys, especially in low grounds. An account appeared anonymously in a Quebec paper, as follows: —

Rivière Ouelle, 17 *Octobre*, 1860.

"Ce matin trois fortes secousses de tremblement de terre sont venues jeter la frayeur au milieu de nos populations.

"Les bâtisses situées de chaque côté de notre rivière ont souffert généralement. [Dix-huit cheminées ont été renversées.] La croix de notre église et le coq sur qui la montait sont à terre; les murs de notre belle église sont lézardés. Les secousses étaient effrayantes; la première, la plus violente, à commencé à six heures et quart, et a duré quatre minutes et quarante secondes, très violentes durant dix secondes et s'affaiblissant graduellement; la secousse la plus faible à six heures et vingt minutes, a duré trois à quatre secondes, et la troisième a commencé a six heures et demie, et n'a duré que deux à trois secondes; mais, comme la première, c'était un choc saccadé faisant danser les meubles, décrochant les cadres, les horloges, etc.

"Les secousses ont été plus faibles sur les hauteurs, que dans les plaines, de sorte que mes bâtisses se sont trouvées à l'abri des accidents.

"Jamais de mémoire de nos habitants, nous n'avons eu des coups aussi forts. Je suis demeuré devant mon horloge tout le temps pour m'assurer de sá durée. * * * Un bruit sourd et fort nous a d'abord averti et ensuite sont venus les secousses et les craquements."

Eboulements, near Murray Bay, 5^h 36′ A.M. Violent. Five other feeble shocks in rapid succession, another at noon, and another at 5^h P.M. This is the only place where these latter shocks are mentioned, but the hour of the first is probably an error.

Bay St. Paul, 5^h 50′ A.M. Violent shock; chimneys fell.

St. Thomas (Montmagny), 6^h A.M. Two shocks.

St. Joseph de la Beauce; 6^h 10′ A.M.

Quebec, 5^h 50′ A.M. Several shocks, not so severe as at Rivière Ouelle, but especially marked in the low grounds.

Leeds, Megantic, 6^h 10′ to 6^h 15′ A.M.

Richmond, 5^h 45′ A.M.

Three Rivers, about 6^h A.M. Shocks felt for two minutes.

Granby, about 6^h A.M.

St. Hyacinthe, 5^h 45′ A.M. Three shocks continuing more than a minute; buildings reported damaged.

Maskinonge, 6^h A.M. Shocks felt for more than a minute. Supposed to be from north to south.

Montreal, 5^h 50′ A.M. Two or three perceptible shocks, felt less on the mountain than on lower ground.

St. Martin, Isle Jesus, 5^h 55′. At Dr. Smallwood's observatory, two distinct and smart shocks. The wave passed from east to west. Barometer 29.964 inches, temperature 40.3, wind N. E., cloudy.

Cornwall, 6^h A.M.

Prescott, 5^h 30′.

Belleville, 5^h 30′. One shock. This place is about 9° of longitude west of Bic.

Hamilton, 4^h 45′ A.M.

In all, or nearly all, of these places the usual rumbling noise preceded the shock, and gradually decreased as it passed. The shock was felt on the Atlantic coast. At Saco, Maine, there was a strong shock. This earthquake was felt as far west as Auburn, in New York, and south to Newark, New Jersey.[1] In Maine, New Hampshire, Vermont and Massachusetts, four light shocks were felt from east to west, with a feeble, subterranean noise.

In *March*, there were two shocks in Massachusetts, according to some reports.[2] 1861.
July 12, about 9 P.M., a shock was felt at Montreal, Ottawa, Prescott, Ogdensburg, Brockville, Saint Andrews and St. Johns, but it was most violent at Ottawa, where it over-

[1] Silliman's Journal (2), vol. xxx, p. 150.

[2] New York Weekly Herald, March 9. Bunker Hill Aurora.

turned chimneys. According to Professor Dawson, it was, in several places, preceded by a dull noise, then a series of light vibrations, which were terminated by a sudden shock. At Prescott, three shocks were reported.[1] At $9^h\ 3'$ a strong shock was felt at Isle Jesus, lasting twenty seconds, and apparently coming from the north-north-west.[2] This earthquake was also felt at Syracuse, New York, where it lasted four seconds, shaking furniture. The date of this shock has been much confused; Perrey places the New York shock on the tenth, and another report gives the eleventh for the disturbance at Isle Jesus. They were all doubtless to be referred to one.

August 31, at $5^h\ 22'$ A.M., two shocks were felt at Washington, at an interval of about five seconds, and each lasted six or seven seconds. The direction seemed to be south to north, and they were felt at Cincinnati, Ohio.

1862. *February* 2, 1862, about 8^h P.M., a strong shock at Colchester, Connecticut; service in the churches was interrupted; at Lyme it lasted three or four seconds. This is in the region of which East Haddam is the centre.

February 4, about $7^h\ 30'$ A.M., at Saybrook, and other towns in Middlesex County, Massachusetts, a shock less than that two days before lasted some seconds.

1864. April 20, 1864, between 1^h and 2^h P.M, a shock more violent than that of 1860 was felt at Quebec but not noticed at Montreal. Two shocks were felt at Danville and Father Point. The time at Quebec was probably $1^h\ 10' - 1^h\ 15'$ P.M., and two distinct shocks of five or six seconds duration, were noticed. In the Harvey Hill Mines, at a depth of 180 feet, it was perceptible. At Father Point, another shock at 11^h P.M. is reported.[3]

October 21, $4^h\ 10'$ A.M., four distinct shocks were felt at Montreal. They seemed to come from the east, and each lasted about ten seconds.

1867. *December* 18, 1867, 3^h A.M., a shock is reported in New York and Vermont, as far south as Whitehall, on the boundary of these States; and in British America, from Belleville, Canada, to Sackville, New Brunswick. It lasted about twenty-five seconds. At Burlington, Vermont, most of the inhabitants were waked up. At Syracuse, at $3^h\ 10'$, and the duration estimated at $1'\ 30''$; direction from south to north, stronger at the commencement than the end. At Ogdensburg, the noise seemed to last two minutes and the vibrations one minute; direction west to east; intensity varying gradually, highest at either extreme. At Hammond, the first shock is said to have occurred at $2^h\ 50'$ A.M., and was followed by others lighter. At $4^h\ 27'$ a final shock. At Montreal, at 3^h A.M. The shock extended from Port Hope on the west, to Trois Rivières on the east.[4]

[As nearly two years have elapsed since this paper was prepared, it has been thought best to continue the enumeration of earthquakes in New England up to the time of publication.]

1869. *October* 22, about 6^h A.M., an earthquake was felt over New England, and the eastern Province. In Nova Scotia it was noticed at Halifax, Kentville and Annapolis. At St. John, New Brunswick, the shock was severe, lasting about $20''$, and preceded by a rumbling noise. People were frightened from their houses. At Frederickton, chimneys were thrown down and walls cracked. At New Haven, very few noticed it, and it was even less at Boston.[5]

[1] Canadian Naturalist and Geologist, vol. VI, p. 329.
[2] *Ibid*, vol. VII, p. 43.
[3] *Ibid*, New Series, vol. I, p. 156.
[4] Silliman's Journal (2), vol. XLV, p. 135.
[5] Silliman's Journal (2), vol. XLVIII, p. 418.

October 20, 1870, at 11^h 25′ a distinct vibration was felt from New Brunswick to Iowa. The duration and direction of the shock have been variously stated, and illustrate the difficulty of seismic observations, without instruments. By my own observations, the duration was more than a minute. I was seated at a very solid desk, and when the shock commenced was writing, which became impossible, and on looking at my watch, I found that the vibration continued sensibly 43″, but died away so gradually that I could not distinguish it from possible jar from passing teams. No noise could be observed. All persons familiar with earthquakes, know the peculiar feeling of direction, almost indescribable, and very various; sometimes like a train of cars passing under a bridge, but so distinct that the noise or vibration comes from a certain direction. In the present case, the shock, although slight, was sufficient to move a door of my desk that happened to be open, its plane in a south-south-east direction, through an arc of 4°-6° repeatedly and rapidly, indicating a course of, approximately, north-north-east to south-south-west. An observer in the same neighborhood thought the oscillation was from south-south-west to north-north-east, and the duration about 28″. 1870.

Many persons in Boston felt a slight nausea, while others did not feel the shock at all. It was felt less on the new-made lands than in the ancient part of the city. In Canada the effects were more severe and walls are reported cracked, and chimneys overthrown. A telegraph operator in Quebec was in the act of enquiring about the earthquake at Montreal, when it was felt at the latter place.

At Portland, Maine, glass was broken; the shock was felt more perceptibly on the wharves. The telegraph operator at Bangor reported the shock about 2″ before it was felt at Portland. About three hundred feet of the Ogdensburg Railroad, sixteen miles from the city, settled ten feet at the time of the earthquake.

At Bath the vibrations seemed east and west, and their duration 15″.

At Bowdoin College, Brunswick, a chimney was broken; the direction seemed north-east and south-west, and the duration 30″- 40″.

Augusta, two shocks were noticed; the duration was 25″.

Lewiston, bricks were thrown from several chimneys, and the shock lasted about 30″.

Burlington, Vermont, a distinct shock at 11^h 26′ A.M. There were regular vibrations from south to north, lasting in all about 15″.

Newburyport, Massachusetts, a slight jar was felt, which was immediately followed by a heavy rumbling lasting 30″, jarring buildings and ringing doorbells. It seemed to pass off in a south-westerly direction.

At Cambridge, Massachusetts, Professor Winlock, of the Observatory, considered the direction of the vibrations about 10° north of east, but he judged only from the appearance of the sides of a vessel containing milk.

At Boston, an observer gives the time of the cessation of the shock at 11^h 25′ 37″ Cambridge mean time.

At Springfield, three distinct shocks were noticed, of which the last was the severest, lasting 7″- 8″.

At New Haven, Connecticut, and other places, there were two distinct series of vibrations. The shock commenced at 11^h 19′ 45″ New Haven mean time, or 1′ 45″ after it reached Boston, apparently. It lasted ten seconds, and the individual half vibration, lasted about two-thirds of a second; after an interval of five seconds there was another shock, like the first, of eleven seconds duration. It was thought that the direction was north-north-east to south-south-west. Another report gives the direction as from north-east to south-west, and the duration 20″. Hartford, the shock lasted from 20″–60″, and the wave apparently moved from north-west to south-east.

At Albany, New York, Professor Hough, of the Dudley Observatory, gives the time at 11^h 15′, and the duration 1′. A rumbling noise was heard, and a clock pendulum swinging north and south was made to vibrate east and west. Since 9^h A.M. of the previous day, the barometer had fallen rapidly .7 of an inch. During the shock the mercury in the registering barometer was violently agitated.

At Cleveland, Ohio, several clocks were stopped, each indicating nearly 11^h 45′ A.M. Slight shocks were felt at Richmond, Virginia, and at Dubuque, Iowa.[1]

There were no seismometers in any observatory in New England, and we are again compelled to infer roughly the direction and force.

It was intended when this enumeration of the New England earthquakes was prepared, to supplement it by a full discussion of the geological features of the regions where these have been most frequent and severe, and also by a map of such of the so-called trap regions of New England and the adjacent parts of Canada, as present distinct indications of volcanic origin. Our State Reports have very frequently been prepared by those who, with an admirable knowledge of general geology, have been deficient in the familiarity with volcanic remains, which only a careful study of both the active and extinct systems of volcanoes can furnish. It is probable that the very general, and much abused term "trap" has been given to indurated and obscure aqueous deposits; certainly, not enough care has been exercised in distinguishing the various kinds which occur in our well-known dikes and veins.

Although nearly a century ago attention was called to the phenomena observed at West River Mountain, on the Connecticut River, in New Hampshire,[2] yet no vulcanologist (if this term may be used), has ever examined the mountain, although, if the reports then published were correct, masses of slag, rapilli and scoria were abundant, at or near the crater-like summit. Montreal has been called an ancient trachytic cone. Gay Head, on Martha's Vineyard, and the Moodus Hill, in Connecticut, have had their volcanic nature affirmed, and denied. And the whole valley of the Connecticut River, seamed with dikes and dotted with eruptive cones, is unstudied as yet. No doubt exists that volcanic agencies have been at work here, in comparatively recent times, for the hardened marble of the Vermont beds on either side of dikes, show the hot rock was an intruder on the limestone deposits. The dikes in the conglomerate, near Boston, show the same subsequent date for some of these formations.

When Mr. Percival attempted to report on the geology of Connecticut, he was much impressed with the remarkable and frequent trap ridges and dikes in the centre of the

[1] Silliman's Journal (2), vol. L, p. 434.

[2] Memoirs American Academy, vol. I (1), p. 312. In Dr. Dwight's Travels, is the following: — "At Hinsdale, on the Connecticut River, in the State of New Hampshire, was an eruption of fire in 1752, from a volcanic mountain, called West River Mountain. This miniature eruption was accompanied by a loud noise, resembling the sound of a cannon. A hole was found about six inches in diameter; a pine tree which stood near it, was partially covered by a black mineral substance, forced out of the passage, consisting chiefly of melted and calcined iron ore, and strongly resembling the scoria of a blacksmith forge."

State. He had never seen a volcano, but the curiously radiating ridges, and semi-circular mounds and depressions, suggested a common origin, and that volcanic.

Our geologists are now prosecuting their examinations into the physical geology of New England, in a way unknown when most of the State reports were published; and, although the purpose with which this paper was commenced has been necessarily abandoned for the present, yet these most interesting localities may be examined by those now in the field, and useful results expected.

The regions indicated by the earthquakes catalogued, are as follows: —

1. A region in Canada, somewhat elliptical in form, with the city of Montreal at its western focus.

2. A region around the mouth of the Merrimack River, in New Hampshire and Massachusetts, and extending to Boston.

3. A region smaller than either of the others, around New Haven, Lyme and East Haddam.

These are, as will be seen, comparatively independent, although a severe shock may be simultaneous in all. The trap indications (and the word trap is here used in its popular signification, to mean any felspathic, igneous rocks, containing much augite and hornblende,) are more continuous, and are also widely diffused. Northern Vermont, the Connecticut valley, central Connecticut, and eastern Massachusetts, are in some sort distinct, although not differing so much as to be referred to different ages; for it seems probable that the dikes have been formed at intervals in the same locality, and their formation may be, and doubtless is, now going on from time to time, at various depths below the surface, and by the high temperature they bring in contact with the cold rock, through which they break, or into whose cavities they run, produce the tremors and disturbances we call earthquakes.

TABULAR VIEW OF NEW ENGLAND EARTHQUAKES.

DATE.			EXTENT.		COURSE.
1568			Eastern Connecticut and Rhode Island. These four are Indian traditions, reported by Roger Williams. See p. 14.		
1574					
1584					
1592					
1638	June 1	2^h–4^h P.M.	All New England: quite severe.		NW–SE
1642	March 5	7^h A.M.			
	June 1	1^h P.M.	Massachusetts.		E–W
1653	Oct. 29				
1658	April (4?)		New England; violent.		
1660	Jan. 31				
1662	Jan. 26	6^h P.M.	New England.	* * *	
	Nov. 6				
1663	Jan. 26	5^h 30′ P.M.	Canada and New England.		
	Jan. 28	9^h A.M.			
1665	Feb. 24		Canada; slight in New England.		
	Oct. 15	9^h 30′			
1668					
1669					
1670					
1706					
1720	Jan. 8				
1727	Feb. 29	10^h 40′ P.M.	Centring near the mouth of the Merrimack.	* * * *	NW–SE
	Nov. 7	11^h P.M.	Newbury; all slight and attended with noise.		

1727	Nov. 12	$3^h\,30'$ P.M.	Newbury; all slight and attended with noise.		
	Nov. 12	$4^h\,30'$ P.M.	"		
	Nov. 13		"		
	Jan. 3	9^h P.M.	"		
	Jan. 6	9^h P.M.	"		
	Jan. 24	$9^h\,30'$ P.M.	"		
	Jan. 28	$6^h\,30'$ A.M.	"		
	Jan. 28	10^h A.M.	"		
	Jan. 29	1^h A.M.	"		
	Jan. 30	2^h P.M.	"		
	Feb. 21	$12^h\,30'$ A.M.	"		
	Feb. 29		"		
	March 17	3^h A.M.	"		
	March 19	$1^h\,40'$ P.M.	"		
	March 19	9^h P.M.	"		
1728	April 28	5^h P.M.	"		
	May 12	$9^h\,40'$ P.M.	"		
	May 17	8^h P.M.	"		
	May 22	10^h A.M.	"		
	June 6	3^h A.M.	"		
	June 8	3^h A.M.	"		
	June 11	9^h A.M.	"		
	July 3	2^h A.M.	"		
	July 23		"		
	Jan. 30	2^h P.M.	A distinct shock at Boston.	* *	
	March 19	$2^h\,30'$ P.M.	Newbury.		
1729	Sept. 8	$3^h\,30'$ (?)	"		
	Sept. 29	$4^h\,30'$ P.M.	"		
	Oct. 29	$10^h\,40'$ P.M.	"		
	Nov. 14	8^h A.M.	"	* *	
	Nov. 27	8^h P.M.	"		
	Feb. 8	8^h P.M.	"		
	Feb. 8	12^h M.	"		
	Feb. 26	$1^h\,45'$ A.M.	"	* *	
1730	April 12	8^h P.M.	"		
	July 28	9^h A.M.	"		
	Aug. 15	8^h A.M.	"	* *	
	Nov. 6		"		
	Nov. 14	9^h A.M.	"		
	Nov. 25	$8^h\,20'$ P.M.	"		
	Dec. 6	$10^h\,45'$ P.M.	"		
	Dec. 11	$6^h\,45'$ P.M.	"		
	Dec. 12	$10^h\,30'$ P.M.	" No noise, but felt at Boston.	—	
	Jan. 7	7^h P.M.	"		
	Jan. 7	M.	"		
	March 7	5^h P.M.	"		
1731	May 28	9^h A.M.	"		
	July 5	- A.M.	"		
	Aug. 21	9^h P.M.	"		
	Oct. 1	11^h P.M.	"		
	Feb. 7	7^h P.M.	"		
1732	Sept. 5	11^h A.M.	" No noise, but felt at Boston and Montreal.	—	
	Dec. 30	— A.M.	"		
	March 1		"		
1733	Oct. 19	M.	"		
	Jan. 16	$10^h\,20'$ P.M.	"		
1734	June 29	$3^h\,15'$ P.M.	"		
	Oct. 9	$10^h\,20'$ A.M.	"		
	Nov. 11-12	M.	"		
	Nov. 16	6^h A.M.	"		
	Feb. 2	$5^h\,45'$ P.M.	"		
	March 21	$10^h\,30'$ A.M.	"		
1736	July 13	$9^h\,45'$ A.M.	"	* *	
	Oct. 1	$1^h\,30'$ A.M	"		
	Nov. 12	2^h A.M.	"		
	Nov. 12	6^h A.M.	"		
	Feb. 6	$4^h\,15'$ P.M.	" Shocks felt at Boston at $4^h\,30'$ P.M.		
1737	Sept. 9	$10^h\,20'$	"		
	Dec. 7	11^h P.M.	" Felt at New York and Boston.	* * *	
1739	Aug. 2	$2^h\,30'$ A.M.	"		
1740	Dec. 14	$6^h\,35'$ A.M.	"		
	Jan. 18	4^h A.M.	"		
	Jan. 25	$3^h\,50'$ P.M.	"		
N. S. 1741	Dec. 6	8^h A.M.	Boston and vicinity.	—	

1741	June 13	10^{h} 35′ A.M.			
1744	May 16		Quebec.		
	June 3		Cambridge.		
	Dec. 23	M.	Newbury.		
1746	Feb. 2	9^{h}–10^{h} P.M.	Boston.		
1755	Nov. 18	4^{h} 11′ 35″ A.M.	All New England.	* * * *	NW–SE
	Nov. 18	5^{h} 29′			
	Nov. 22	8^{h} 27′ P.M.	Boston.		
	Dec. 19	10^{h} P.M.	"		
1756	Jan. 2		"		
	Nov. 16	4^{h} A.M.	"		
	Dec. 4	10^{h} P.M.	"		
1757	July 8	2^{h} 15′ P.M.	"		
1758	April 24	9^{h} 30′ P.M.	Pennsylvania and Maryland; slight in New England.		
1759	Feb. 2		Boston.		
1760	Feb. 3		New England.		
	Nov. 9		Boston; more severe in the neighborhood.		
1761	Feb. –		"		
	March 12	2^{h} 15′ A.M.	New England.		
	March 16				
	Nov. 1	8^{h} P.M.	Massachusetts and New Hampshire.	—	NW–SE
1766	Feb. 2		Massachusetts and Rhode Island.	—	
	June 14		Essex County, Mass.		
	Aug. 25		Newport, R. I.		
	Dec. 17	6^{h} 48′	Portsmouth, N. H.		
1783	Nov. 29	10^{h} 50′ P.M.	New England and as far as Pennsylvania.		N–S
1785	Jan. 2	7^{h} 15′ A.M.	Cambridge; and about the same time at Baltimore.		
1786	Nov. 29	4^{h} P.M.	"		
1787	Feb. 25	1^{h} A.M.	"		
1791	May 16	8^{h} A.M.	East Haddam, Conn.	* *	
	May 17	– P.M.	"		
	May 18	10^{h} P.M.	" Also from Boston to Philadelphia.		W–E
	December		Canada.		
1792	Aug. 28	10^{h} P.M.	East Haddam.		
	Oct. 24	1^{h} A.M.	"	* * *	
1793	Jan. 11	8^{h} A.M.	"		
	July 6	6^{h} A.M.	"		
1704	March 6	2^{h} P.M.	"	* *	
	March 6	11^{h} P.M.	"		
1800	Dec. 25		Newport, Boston, Concord and elsewhere.		
	Nov. 11-12		Boston.		
1801	March 1		Salem.		
1805	Aug. 11	7^{h} P.M.	East Haddam.	* *	
	Dec. 30	6^{h} A.M.	"		
1810	Nov. 9	9^{h} 15′ P.M.	Exeter, N. H., and northward.		NW–SE
1812	Feb. 9	9^{h} A.M.	East Haddam.	* *	
	July 5	8^{h} A.M.	"		
1813	Dec. 28	4^{h} P.M.	"		
1816	Sept. 9		Montreal; hardly noticed in central New England.		
	Sept. 16				
1817	Oct. 5		Woburn, Mass.		
1818	Oct. 11		Quebec.		
1819	November		Montreal.		
1821	February		Quebec.		
1824	July 9		New Brunswick.		
1827	Aug. 23		New London, Conn.		
1828	Aug. 20		Canada.		
1829	January		Portsmouth, N. H.		
1831	July 14		Murray Bay, Canada.		
1833	March		"		
	April		"		
1837	April 12		Hartford, Conn.		
1840	Aug. 9		New Haven and northward.		NW–SE
	Sept. 10		Hamilton, Canada.		W–E
1841	Jan. 25	– A.M.	New York State.		W–E
1842	Nov. 9		Montreal.		
1845	Oct. 26		New York and western New England		
1846	May 30	1^{h} 30′ P.M.	Newburyport and Salem.		
	July 10		Deerfield, N. H.		
	Sept. 12	Sunset.	"		
	Oct. 29	9^{h} P.M.	"		
	Oct. 31	– P.M.	"		
	Dec. 2		"		
1847	Jan. 8	3^{h} P.M.			
	Jan. 11	11^{h} 30′ P.M.	Albany, N. Y.		

1847	Feb. 2		Deerfield, N. H.		
	Feb. 14		Meredith Village, N. H.		
	Feb. 19		Belfast, Me.		
	Feb. 21		Deerfield, N. H.		
	April 1	9^h P.M.	Limington, Me.		
	June 9		Lake Winnepiseogee, N. H.		
	July 9		Glens Falls.		
	Aug. 8	10^h A.M.	Boston and towards Cape Cod.		
1848	Jan. 1		Nova Scotia.		
	Feb. 1		"		
	May 23		Montreal.		
	Sept. 9	10^h P.M.	Southern New England, to Pennsylvania.		
	Nov. 6	6^h 15′ A.M.	Grand Island, Canada.		
	Dec. 11	3^h A.M.	Montreal.		
1849	Feb. 4		Newport, R. I.		
	Feb. 15		Springfield, Mass., and eastern New York.		
	Oct. 8	– P.M.	Middlesex County, Mass.		
1850	July 20	– P.M.	Portland, Me.		
1851	Jan. 3		Waterville, Me.		
	Jan. 30	5^h P.M.	Canada.		
1852	Jan. 10	6^h 40′ A.M.	Massachusetts.		
	Feb. 11	5^h 40′ A.M.	Canada.	—	WNW-ESE
	April 30	– P.M.	New England; more at Washington, D.C.	—	
	June 30		Claremont, N. H.		
	Aug. 1		Groton, Conn.		
	Aug. 2	11^h P.M.	New Brunswick.		
	Aug. 11	– P.M.	Deerfield, Mass.	—	
	Nov. 27	11^h 45′ P.M	Newburyport, Mass.		
1853	March 12	2^h–3^h A.M.	New York and Canada.		W–E
	May 24		Canada.		
	June 3		Nova Scotia.	* * *	
	July 17	5^h–6^h A.M.	Portland, Me.	* *	
	Sept. 7	11^h 10′ P.M.	New Bedford, Mass.		
1854	Feb. 22-23	M.	Reading, Mass.		W–E
	October		Keene, N.H.	—	
	Dec. 4	10^h P.M.	Canada.		
	Dec. 10	12^h 30′ P.M.	Newburyport, Mass.		
1855	Feb. 8		New England.	—	
	Feb. 19		Maine.	—	
1856	May 1		Canada.	—	
	Dec. 28		"	—	
1857	October		"		
1858	May 10		"		
	May 17	3^h P.M.	"		NW–SE
	June 30	10^h 45′ P.M.	New Haven, Conn.		
	Oct. 8	3^h 15′ P.M.	New York and Canada.		
1859			Canada.		
1860	March 16	9^h 30′ P.M.	Provincetown, Mass.		
	March 16	10^h 15′ P.M.	"		
	Oct. 17	6^h A.M.	Canada and Northern States.		E–W
1861	March		Massachusetts.		WNW-SSE
	July 12	9^h P.M.	Canada.		
1862	Feb. 2	8^h P.M.	Connecticut.	—	
	Feb. 4	7^h 30′ A.M.	Middlesex Co., Mass.	—	
1864	April 20	1^h–2^h P.M.	Quebec and Montreal.		
	April 20	11^h P.M.	Father Point.	* *	
	Oct. 21	4^h 10′ A.M.	Montreal.	* * * *	E–W
1867	Dec. 18	3^h A.M.	Vermont and Canada.		W–E S–N
1869	Oct. 22	6^h A.M.	New England and Canada.	—	
1870	Oct. 20	11^h 25′ A.M.	New England and westward.	—	NNE-SSW

Distributed by months the earthquakes occurred as follows :

In October, 19; November, 29; December, 22; January, 20; February, 36; March, 22. Winter months . . 148
April, 9; May, 13; June, 14; July, 13; August, 15; September, 10. Summer months 74
No month given 9

Total, 231

Published January, 1871.

www.ingramcontent.com/pod-product-compliance
Lightning Source LLC
LaVergne TN
LVHW011138110826
845150LV00008B/2396

* 9 7 8 1 4 1 8 1 9 3 3 2 4 *